Scoping

The science and art of defining, estimating, documenting and planning cyber security assessments

by
Andreas Aaris-Larsen

First published April 2025

Revision 1.0

Copyright © 2025 Andreas Aaris-Larsen

All rights reserved.

ISBN: 9798391627661

Foreword

At its core, scoping is the process of identifying the work that needs to be carried out. As a cyber security consultant, whether this be as an independent working on your own, or as part of a larger consultancy with a dedicated sales function, internal or external to the clients' company, scoping is almost universally the first activity that requires your care and attention. Paradoxically, it is generally also the activity with which you are entrusted only at the later stages of your professional development. The reasoning for this is traditionally given with arguments such as "it's an art, not a calculus" and "it takes a lot of experience to get right". I argue that this need not be the case.

While there are many different approaches to scoping a cyber security assessment and related projects, the subject is generally not well-understood by most practitioners within the field. This applies both to the sales staff trying to sell these consulting services, and to the consultants using the scope to deliver the requested services. The subject by its very nature can be hard to teach, in that the environments and solutions which consultants are being asked to scope, are diverse and ever-changing. And the human element (the client presenting the solution) and their motivation can likewise vary vastly, as can the internal politics and company-specific requirements that are at play.

But that should not be a reason to not teach or train on this subject.

Scoping can be a struggle for even the best of us. But it shouldn't have to be. The existing literature on this subject is either generic one-pagers on corporate websites, designed to put prospective buyers at ease, or massive tomes of in-depth psychological manuals on different approaches to behavioural design, conflict resolution and non-verbal communication and persuasion. Technical-minded security consultants, while they can for sure benefit from absorbing that material, need subject-specific tools and methodologies to scope effectively and with confidence. Ask any consultant who just experienced a failed project, and they will likely tell you that the cascades of failures experienced started at the very beginning, or rather before the beginning, with the scope.

That is why I wrote this book. The experience gained from thousands of scoping calls (literally, I counted), meetings and writeups, distilled into five key questions that will hopefully lead to a better scoping experience for you, the client, and everyone else involved, and ultimately provide value to all parties involved. And for those on the client-side, provide an in-depth look at what to expect when requesting a scoping-session with a cyber security consultant.

This is a book for security consultants, written by a security consultant. I hope it helps, and I hope you enjoy it.

About the author

Andreas has been a jack-of-all-trades within the security consultancy space for more than a decade, with experience in attack and penetration testing with solid knowledge about the tactical, operational, threat modelling and project management aspects of international information security projects.

From doing commodity vulnerability scanning to advising regulatory bodies on the implementation and verification of security standards, from traditional infrastructure and web application testing to targeted threat emulation, from architectural and design advisory work to digital forensics and incident response. He has worked with the majority of banks and financial institutions in Scandinavia, as well as internationally, gambling and trading services throughout Europe, and critical infrastructure and manufacturing companies of all sizes. He has conducted investigations ranging from simple ransomware infestations to organised industrial espionage and geopolitically motivated incidents by nation-backed actors.

Andreas has also taught M.Sc. level courses on security assessments and consultancy at the Department of Applied Mathematics and Computer Science at the Technical University of Denmark (DTU), as well as multiple secure development courses for banking clients across the Nordics. For the last five years of his tenure there. Andreas has also been a part of the F-Secure/WithSecure Academy programme, employing and teaching university graduates and new-comers to the security industry the technical and soft skills required to operate in the world of cyber security consultancy.

Through this expansive and varied experience, Andreas has accrued a breadth of knowledge that is rare in this space, where it seems that new areas of expertise pop up almost daily. As such, he is able to interact with and appreciate security concerns at most levels of an organisation, and within most industries.

Most relevant to this book, Andreas has in his previous work studied, developed and aligned the scoping practices of a global consultancy business through the absorption of four companies spread across differing cultural, legal and geographical locations. This has mainly focused on consultancy within the financial sector and with world-leading brands, often involving stakeholders ranging from developers and project managers to business owners and board of directors.

Andreas currently serves as Principal Consultant at Banshie Cyber Security Services, and primarily engages in incident response and digital forensics, as well as targeted attacks and threat actor emulation projects, while coaching and supporting new team members earning their stripes in the industry.

Table of Contents

1. The statement of work 1
    Proposal 2
        Value proposition 2
        Account team 4
        Financial overview 6
        Legal requirements 6
    Statement of Work 7
        Describing the target 7
        Defining the approach 8
    Scope 10
    Combined 11
2. Why 16
    Alignment 17
    Legal 20
        When can you test a web application? 21
        When can you test a mobile app? 21
        Does the application owner also own the server that it runs on? 21
    Cost and responsibilities 23
    Practicalities 24
3. What 25
4. Who 37
    A word on Quality Assurance 38
5. When 39
6. How 42
    How to run a scoping meeting 42
        The invite 43
        The meeting 46
            Language 47
            Scoping questions 51
            Dealing with hostility 55
            Ending the meeting 58

- Estimating and planning 60
  - Calculus and scoping models 60
    - Statistics 61
    - Time-boxed 64
    - Representative testing 66
    - Programme or advisory work 66
  - Pre-requisites 67
  - Pre-mortem 68
    - Applying Pre-Mortem to Improve Scoping and Estimation 69
    - Benefits 69
- Writing it all up 70

7. Closing thoughts 71
A Final Thank You 72

1. The statement of work
The paper that governs your professional life

Whatever name is given to this document, the work of a cyber security consultant starts with some form of communication in which the client makes their wishes known. These are then reflected back to the client in the form of a contractual document, which is eventually signed, and the work can commence. This applies to security practitioners working internally within a company, such as within quality assurance teams, compliance functions, or internal red teams or other offensive services, as well as those external to the company. While the level of detail and the way in which the document is used may differ depending on which category you find yourself in, the overall content and structure and reasoning behind it will remain consistent.

This document is commonly referred to as the proposal, the statement of work, or simply the scope. This can be in the form of a single document, or it can be split into several, each with its own benefits and challenges. The benefit of splitting the document is that each can be signed in isolation. For instance, the financial contract can be signed by a procurement department with reference to the Statement of Work or Scope, and still be legally binding as long as the finances outlined in the Proposal remain unaltered. If changes are made to any other part of the project, such as dates, system names, or the addition or removal of minor components that otherwise do not alter the estimated effort, the proposal does not need to revisit a procurement process, and those sections can be signed off on by project owners, system owners, or similar technical contacts. The downside is, of course, that managing multiple documents adds complexity and introduces additional risks of mistakes.

Whether split into multiple documents or a single monolithic one, any such document or documents should contain the sections described in the following.

Proposal

At its core, the proposal is largely a legal and financial document describing the cost and breakdown of the proposed project, as well as what terms and conditions will govern the contract. As such, it is largely something written by sales staff, with input provided by technical experts if and when needed.

Value proposition

The proposal should start with presenting its value proposition. A value proposition in the context of a proposal is a statement that answers why someone should do business with you. It should convince a potential customer why your service or product will be of more **value** to them than similar offerings from your competition, and it should explain why the whole project experience will be smoother with you than with anyone else.

This can be presented without going into the details of the project at hand, but simply highlighting how you have the right technical knowledge, the industry experience, the secret sauce, etc. However, for maximum effect the value proposition can, and probably should, be tailored to fit with the specifics of the project. The following is an example of a fictitious proposition, although it is based on an actual gambling provider, where compliance and financial experience is equally important as technical knowledge.

In this and the following such examples, the client name will be given as ACME, and the name of our consultancy will be simply ConsultingCompany.

ACME is in the process of developing a new management component for their gaming system, and requires assurances that the solution is resistant to modern attack vectors as well as internal security threats.

ConsultingCompany is uniquely positioned to support this work, and have extensive experience within the gaming and gambling industry. ConsultingCompany has delivered security assessment and consulting services to ACME since 2011, and as such are familiar with internal ACME processes, the infrastructure and application landscape, as well as the overall IT estate.

ACME is subject to the National Gambling Act of 2012 and the technical requirements and compliance programme of the National Gambling Authority. ConsultingCompany was part of the workgroup that helped the National Gambling Authority create and ratify this programme, and was the sole auditor and accredited security assessor in the first years of the law being in effect. As such, ConsultingCompany is intimately familiar with the requirements ACME is subject to, and brings a wealth of experience from similar organisations.

Additionally, ConsultingCompany holds specialist certifications such as ACAMS Certified Anti-Money Laundering Specialist, and employs PCI DSS Qualified Security Assessors for related work with clients in the financial industry. ConsultingCompany also holds highly technical certifications from industry-recognised bodies such as SANS, CREST, ISC2 and Offensive Security. These include OSCE, OSCP, OSWE, CISSP, CISSM, GPEN, GWAP, GCFA, GREM, GCNA and CCSAS.

ConsultingCompany's primary offering is security consulting services and security testing of critical infrastructure systems, large-volume trading applications, commodity and custom-developed web application and services.

ConsultingCompany will provide a dedicated account team to support ACME throughout the engagement, and will ensure continuity in testing by ensuring that the same consultant team is involved in the project throughout.

Figure 1 - Example value proposition

Please note that this example might be a bit excessive in size, for the purpose of including multiple examples of differentiators that make you stand out to the client. Adjust and refine as needed based on your experience with or knowledge of the client. This example will be discussed in more detail in chapter 6.

This should not be seen as an overly convoluted exercise in executive writing, but rather as a one-off investment, as the qualities that make you stand out from the competition should hopefully be fairly consistent. As such, you should be able to write a value proposition for each of your clients, <u>once</u>, and then re-use that with minor alterations from one project to the next. If you are dealing primarily with clients in a specific vertical, you may even be able to produce a proposition that effectively spans that entire vertical, reducing the overhead even further, although the investment that is customising your pitch, is usually worth it.

Account team

While this may differ between cultures and regions, and will differ depending on how client accounts are managed, the proposal can often include a section to introduce a dedicated account team. Such a section should include the Key Account Manager, Account Director or similar role that's managing the client, as well as a Project Manager, Engagement Manager or Delivery Manager if such roles exist and are dedicated to the client account. If a named consultant is consistently used for the client account, this person should likewise be included and will often be the same consultant that scoped the assignment. All of these should be introduced with names, roles, contact details as well as a profile picture. This helps humanise the contact even though this may be done entirely through the document.

Employee no. 1
Role
Email
Phone number

Employee no. 2
Role
Email
Phone number

Employee no. 3
Role
Email
Phone number

Employee no. 3
Role
Email
Phone number

Figure 2- Example team contacts and roles

Financial overview

With the introductions out of the way, the proposal should summarise and highlight the financial aspects of the commitment. This could take the form of a simple list of line items, or simple single-paragraph explanations of project subcomponents.

Web application security assessment		1.337
Infrastructure security assessment		1.337
Risk assessment of the introduction of XYZ on the ERT net		1.337
	Total	3.917

Figure 3 - Example cost breakdown

This is also a common place for a breakdown of consulting days to be included and split over each line-item, often referred to as "the effort", but this is equally often listed in the Scope section later in the document.

Legal requirements

Lastly, the proposal should include any local legal requirements, such as listing parties in the agreement, signatures, jurisdictions to govern any disputes, and general contractual terms and conditions. This is largely a job for the lawyers, or something where you rely on industry groups to provide tried-and-tested standards and templates. As such, this is not covered in this book. However, from experience, sections on cancellation terms should be given due focus and thoughts with respect to options for enforcement of such terms and any compensation, as these will invariably come into play from time to time.

Statement of Work

The statement of work can be considered a combination of a worksheet and a value proposition. This section is intended for the consultant to describe to the client the consultants' understanding of the assignment that's been presented, along with a high-level plan for how to achieve the desired outcomes. This serves to convince the client that a mutual understanding of the required work has been achieved, and that the consultant has the necessary knowledge and background to solve the assignment to a satisfactory degree, ultimately leading to the client accepting the project.

Describing the target

This section should start with the consultant describing the solution to be assessed, using a combination of the clients' words from the preceding scoping meeting or received documentation, standard industry terms, and named company services that the client will be familiar with. This should include in layman's terms what the target is (a car, an airplane, a web application, a custom implementation of a pseudo-random number generator, etc.), the business reason for the target being employed by the client, and what the clients' primary concerns are with respect to the target.

> ACME is implementing the ABC product to monitor, deploy and manage the SSL/TLS certificates across the ACME environments. As such, ACME requires assurances regarding the security posture of the ABC product and its current implementation in the ACME test environment.
>
> To provide this, ConsultingCompany will conduct a configuration review of the deployed solution thick client and a web application security assessment of its Internet-exposed web interface and manual review of files accessible on the server configured with the ABC product. Additionally, ConsultingCompany will investigate how the solution employs the ACME protocol and ensure that this aligns with industry best practices and does not expose ACME to additional risks.
>
> The assessment will focus on the following:
>
> - Identifying how the solution communicates with other assets as part of the certificate monitoring and deployment process
> - Determining how the solution generates and stores certificates locally, along with its related secrets management
>
> The objective of the assessment will be to determine if the solution is fit for purpose, or can be made so with additional security hardening, to make it a viable component in ACME's production environment.

Figure 4 - Example target description

This is not only to demonstrate to the client that the consultant understands the context in which the target needs to be assessed, but also to serve as an introduction to any other consultants who might end up delivering the project, as it is not uncommon for the scoping and performing consulting being two different people.

The reason for using the clients' internal terms and any diagrams they have provided, is to invoke a sense of isopraxism. Isopraxism is a neurobehaviour that humans display in which we copy each other in order to make both parties feel safe, and it's part of the process of developing rapport which leads to trust. While this is normally something that is done unconsciously, via speech patterns, body language, tempo, etc., it can actively be done via vocabulary as well. In sales and negotiation training, this is referred to as "mirroring" and can be incredibly effective. Effectively retelling the clients' words back to them is also a way of echoism, a part of active listening, which likewise creates a sense of trust and rapport. Both of these will be discussed further in chapter 6.

Defining the approach

Once the target has been described, the Statement of Work should iterate how the assessment is intended to reach its objectives of addressing the concerns expressed by the client. If the project is aligned with a standard offering of the consultancy, this will likely be your standard service description which describes the high-level methodology being used, standards being adhered to, pre-defined tasks and sub-components that make up the service, etc. The following is an example of such a description for an arbitrary web application assessment.

A web application security assessment involves searching for design flaws, vulnerabilities, and inherent weaknesses in the design. This assessment involves analysing the functionality of the target application and attempting to use it in unintended ways that were not specified during the design process. Such unintended functionality may include unauthorised manipulation and viewing of data, as well as identifying programming or configuration errors.

The assessment activities focuses on these key areas:

- Open-source information gathering
- Application reconnaissance and fingerprinting
- Configuration management
- Data and input validation
- Authentication and authorization model review
- Session management implementation
- Error handling and business logic
- Cryptography of data at rest and in transit
- Dynamic internet application functionalities

In particular for this assessment the emphasis will be on determining the overall security posture of the application, uncover weaknesses and vulnerabilities that could present a risk to the client, ensure compliance with regulatory oversights and company stated baselines and identify compensating controls and suggested mitigation strategies to lower the risk to be within the risk appetite of the client

Figure 5- Example service description

Scope

Where the Statement of Work details the intentions and goals of the project, the scope makes up the legal contract between the client and the person performing the assessment. As such, it needs to rigorously and meticulously describe and define what can and cannot be done during the project. In extremis, this section can be the difference between someone going to prison or not (although this is thankfully something I've only experienced once in my career). With reference to the Statement of Work, the scope must formally specify what is in scope for the project, such as:

- Hostnames
- Applications
- URLs
- IP addresses
- Specific features
- System integrations
- Policies and procedures
- Etc.

While it is common for this section to also include the approach or methodology used, this should largely be redundant after the Statement of Work section, and may simply be reduced to blackbox, whitebox/clearbox or greybox, or omitted entirely.

This section should also explicitly state any related systems or components that for one reason or another are outside the scope of the assessment. This could be for legal or contractual reasons, due to integration with 3rd parties for which permission to test has not been obtained, or features that may incur excessive costs if triggered, etc. The topic of legality will be discussed in more detail in chapter 2.

While this may differ and be a matter of personal preference more than anything else, and in fact varies greatly between companies, the Scope section may also be used to write out the estimated effort of the project, expressed in consultant days or specified with a dated testing window.

Lastly, the Scope should include a list of all necessary pre-requisites needed to ensure (or at least heighten the chance of) a successful engagement, along with any other practicalities. This could for instance include:

- The timely delivery of user credentials
- Whitelisting/allowlisting in firewalls, IPS/IDS etc.
- Physical co-location with developers

- Access badges for onsite work to access relevant areas of the clients premises related to the assessment (for arrival, bathroom, coffee, cigarette breaks etc.
- API or application documentation, including documentation of authentication and authorization mechanisms, API methods, requests and responses with their expected parameters
- Machine-readable specifications such as Swagger or WSDL or Postman files
- Data set that can be used with the target in the appropriate environment, such as client IDs, card numbers etc.
- Sufficiently long timeout value on any authorization token used for testing, or temporary disabling of security features that might hinder automated security testing
- Architecture diagram of the target
- Baselines employed on assets to be assessed
- Source code and configuration files for the target solution
- Contact details of technical persons that can provide explanations on the workings of the application(s) to be tested
- Physical device required for testing in case of embedded systems or mobile solutions

These will of course vary greatly depending on what service you are to deliver, as a normal point-in-time assessment of a component will have a lot of practical requirements, whereas a red team exercise may need more in terms of contacts and escalation points, etc.

Combined

With all these sections now present, we should have a document that states why the client should engage us, demonstrates our understanding of the project and its objectives, sets up the project for success, and supports our consultants in achieving the objectives of the project. With a few changes to the examples shown so far, we'll combine them into one in the following.

Value proposition

ACME is in the process of deploying a new management component for their gaming system, and require assurances that the solution is resistant to modern attack vectors as well as internal security threats.

ConsultingCompany is uniquely positioned to support this work, and have extensive experience within the gaming and gambling industry. ConsultingCompany has delivered security assessment and consulting services to ACME since 2011, and as such are familiar with internal ACME processes, the infrastructure and application landscape, as well as the overall IT estate.

ACME is subject to the National Gambling Act of 2012 and the technical requirements and compliance programme of the National Gambling Authority. ConsultingCompany was part of the workgroup that helped the National Gambling Authority create and ratify this programme, and was the sole auditor and accredited security assessor in the first years of the law being in effect. As such, ConsultingCompany is intimately familiar with the requirements ACME is subject to, and brings a wealth of experience from similar organisations.

Additionally, ConsultingCompany holds specialist certifications such as ACAMS Certified Anti-Money Laundering Specialist, and employs PCI DSS Qualified Security Assessors for related work with clients in the financial industry. ConsultingCompany also holds highly technical certifications from industry-recognised bodies such as SANS, CREST, ISC2 and Offensive Security. These include OSCE, OSCP, OSWE, CISSP, CISSM, GPEN, GWAP, GCFA, GREM, GCNA and CCSAS.

ConsultingCompany's primary offering is security consulting services and security testing of critical infrastructure systems, large-volume trading applications, commodity and custom developed web application and services. ConsultingCompany will provide a dedicated account team to support ACME throughout the engagement, and will ensure continuity in testing by ensuring that the same consultant team is involved in the project throughout.

Account team

ConsultingCompany is pleased to present the proposal at hand, and has formed the following account team to support ACME throughout this and future engagements:

Employee no. 1
Role
Email
Phone number

Employee no. 2
Role
Email
Phone number

Employee no. 3
Role
Email
Phone number

Employee no. 4
Role
Email
Phone number

Effort and cost

Web application security assessment	1.337
Infrastructure security assessment	1.337
Risk assessment of the introduction of XYZ on the ERT net	1.337
Total	3.917

Statement of Work

ACME is implementing the ABC product to monitor, deploy and manage the SSL/TLS certificates across the ACME environments. As such, ACME require assurances regarding the security posture of the ABC product and it's current implementation in the ACME test environment.

To provide this, ConsultingCompany will conduct a configuration review of the deployed solution thick client and a web application security assessment of its Internet-exposed web interface, based on available documentation and manual review of files accessible on the server installed and configured with the ABC product. Additionally, ConsultingCompany will investigate how the solution employs the ACME protocol for deploying certificates and ensure that this aligns with industry best practices and does not expose ACME to additional risks.

The assessment will focus on the following:

- Determining the security posture of the Internet-exposed web interface by conducting a web application security assessment
- Identifying how the solution communicates with other assets as part of the certificate monitoring and deployment process
- Determining how the solution generates and stores certificates locally, along with its related secrets management

Given that web applications are often the primary attack surface for organisations, it is crucial to prioritise their security in order to protect critical business assets. The objective of a web application security assessment is to ensure that the target application incorporates the necessary security controls and robust implementation to safeguard business assets, end users, and the organization's reputation.

A web application security assessment involves searching for design flaws, vulnerabilities, and inherent weaknesses in the design. This assessment involves analysing the functionality of the target application and attempting to use it in unintended ways that were not specified during the design process. Such unintended functionality may include unauthorised manipulation and viewing of data, as well as identifying programming or configuration errors.

The assessment activities focuses on these key areas:

- Application reconnaissance and fingerprinting
- Configuration management
- Data and input validation
- Authentication and authorization model review
- Session management implementation
- Error handling and business logic
- Cryptography of data at rest and in transit
- Dynamic Internet application functionalities

In particular, for this assessment the emphasis will be on determining the overall security posture of the application, uncover weaknesses and vulnerabilities that could present a risk to the client, ensure compliance with regulatory oversights and company stated baselines and identify compensating controls and suggested mitigation strategies to lower the risk to be within the risk appetite of the client. The final objective of the assessment will be to determine if the solution is fit for purpose, or can be made so with additional security hardening, to make it a viable component in ACME's production environment.

Scope

The following components will be in scope for this assessment:

- server2.acme.com - 192.168.42.42
- https://ABC.acme.com

The XYZ feature of ABC accessible at https://ABC.acme.com/dangerousfeature has been deemed out of scope due to INSERT_VALID_REASON and will not be targeted during this assessment.

The assessment will be conducted as a grey-box assessment, as ConsultingCompany will be provided with valid user accounts and detailed system documentation.

Pre-requisites

The following pre-requisites must be delivered prior to the assessment start-date to ensure an effective assessment:

- Application documentation, including documentation of authentication and authorization mechanisms, API methods, requests and responses with their expected parameters
- Data set that can be used with the target in the appropriate environment, such as client IDs, card numbers etc.
- Architecture diagram of the solution

Legal, terms and conditions

<omitted>

This will serve as our example and shared reference. In the following chapters we will explore each component in more detail, along with what to include, how to obtain the needed information, and how to present that in a professional and engaging fashion.

2. Why
Why scoping/SoW are important

So why is it important to scope a project before committing to it? Why can't we just tell the client that we'll do whatever they're asking for, and then get on with it? In this chapter we will go through the multiple and very valid reasons for why spending the time conducting a scoping session and subsequently writing it down, is so important.

Alignment

Do you remember the first time you went to a fancy restaurant? For me it was sometime around 2006 somewhere on the outskirts of London. I ordered a steak, which came with some fancy sauce I'd never heard of before. And that's all it came with. No salad, no carbs, nothing. I had to order a side dish when I got the steak, which of course meant that my steak was cold by the time my side dish arrived. This naturally put a damper on the enjoyment. Now you might think I'm an idiot, but where I was from, it was virtually unheard of that whatever you ordered didn't come as a full meal, and I thought that was the normal way of the world. This is called *normality bias*.

> "Normality bias" refers to a cognitive bias or psychological tendency for individuals to underestimate the possibility of a disaster or unusual event occurring, and to perceive their current situation as being normal or predictable. This bias can lead people to underestimate risks and overestimate the likelihood of things continuing as they always have. This also applies when individuals assume that something they take for granted (fire is hot, grass is green, security assessments require you to have valid credentials, etc.) is obvious to everyone else in a conversation, and therefore neglect to mention it or speak their mind.
>
> When individuals are accustomed to a certain routine, environment, or set of circumstances, they develop a sense of familiarity and assume that things will generally remain stable and predictable. This bias can be observed in various aspects of life, such as personal safety, financial stability, or societal stability.
>
> Normality bias can have both positive and negative effects. On the one hand, it can provide comfort and a sense of stability, helping people maintain a sense of normalcy in their daily lives. However, it can also hinder preparedness and response to potential threats or emergencies, and keep people from speaking up even though they know something is wrong or that they have the perfect solution for a problem being discussed. People may fail to take necessary precautions or make contingency plans because they believe that unusual or disastrous events are unlikely to occur, and avoid mentioning their solution because they assume everyone else will have already thought of it and maybe rejected it because it will not work.
>
> Recognizing and addressing normality bias is important for making informed decisions, and for having the courage to speak up when you have the perfect solution and everyone else is still talking in circles. There's a good chance that you are in fact super smart and no one else thought of it! Worst case scenario? Someone will get to show how smart they are, explain why your idea wouldn't work, and in turn make you smarter. Everybody wins.

Now imagine that your client goes to a consultancy and purchases an assessment. They have the assessment performed, but never receive a report. Or a component was left out of the assessment. Don't you think they would be unhappy with that? This is of course an extreme example (because virtually everything in security consulting results in a report) but there are several other items where your norm might differ from that of your clients. When you test a web application, do you also test the server hosting the application? When you perform a vulnerability scan of a server, do you only check the top 1000 ports? Do you only scan TCP and not UDP? Do you cover IPv6?

Writing down what will and will not be performed as part of the project, what will be delivered, what the expectations should be, describing your own understanding of what the client has told you, and then having them read it, ensures that everyone is aligned, and avoids awkward and uncomfortable situations. It also gives the client a natural opportunity to correct any incorrect assumptions, hopefully leading to a smother project. This is also the best way to avoid what's referred to as *scope creep*.

> "scope creep" refers to the gradual and unauthorized expansion of the project's boundaries, objectives, or deliverables beyond the originally defined scope. It occurs when additional tasks, systems, or targets are included in the assessment without proper authorization or agreement from the relevant stakeholders.
>
> Scope creep can have several negative consequences for a security assessment:
>
> - **Increased time and effort**: The unauthorized inclusion of additional targets or systems can significantly increase the time and effort required to complete the assessment, potentially leading to delays and resource constraints.
> - **Inadequate coverage**: If the assessment team is focused on exploring new targets that were not originally part of the scope, they may inadvertently overlook vulnerabilities or weaknesses in the initial targets, compromising the overall effectiveness of the exercise.
> - **Budget implications**: Scope creep can lead to unexpected costs associated with additional resources, tools, or extended timelines. These expenses may not have been accounted for in the original budget, causing financial strain.
> - **Reduced client satisfaction**: When the assessment deviates from the agreed-upon scope, it can erode trust and satisfaction with the client or stakeholders who expected the assessment to adhere to specific boundaries and deliverables.
>
> To mitigate scope creep in a security assessment and related exercises, it is crucial

to establish a well-defined scope at the outset and maintain effective communication and documentation throughout the project. This includes clearly defining the objectives, targets, systems, and limitations of the assessment, as well as obtaining stakeholder buy-in. Regularly reviewing and assessing scope changes against the project's goals and constraints helps ensure that the exercise stays focused and productive.

Legal

The second reason for performing a scoping session and documenting the scope, is for legal reasons. A common concern amongst security consultants, especially the younger and more conscientious ones, is what they are and aren't allowed to do according to the letter of the law.

The short version; you can do whatever you have written permission to do, assuming it isn't otherwise illegal.

This is the number one reason for why you, as an individual, want the scope written down and confirmed by the client. Of course there are the contractual reasons for having things in writing, stating what services must be delivered to fulfill the contract, and those are good for the business, but the same document serves as your Get Out Of Jail Free card. Because in most instances, if YOU break the law, YOU go to prison, not the people who sold or bought the assessment.

Laws will be different depending on where in the world you are when reading this book, and the goal of this book is not to train you as a lawyer. So rather than try to detail laws for each country I will instead try and distil this into some core concepts, principles and assumptions that should keep you safe regardless of where you find yourself working.

- **Verify ownership** - Only the owner of an asset can give you permission to attack it, even if it's part of a security assessment conducted with the best of intentions. This is why you want to describe exactly what you will and will not be targeting, and have the client confirm that they are in fact the legal owner of all components in scope for the assessment. Always assume that if you access someone else's system, or even attempt to access it, even if you fail, without the expressed permission of the system owner or someone with larger ownership (manager, C-suite, board of directors, etc.), it might be a crime.
- **Write it down** - verbal contracts are (in most places) just as binding as a written one. But a written one is a lot easier to prove
- **If it feels wrong, don't do it**
- **If you think it might be illegal, it probably is**
- **If what you're doing digitally can be compared to something that is illegal when done physically, it's probably illegal** - When no specific "hacker" law exists, common law usually steps in. That means your local law regarding burglary, vandalism, destruction of property, financial crime and so on, applies.
- **Never. Read. Another. Persons. Mail.** - This cannot be overstated. Letter-secrecy laws are one of those laws that tend to be taken very serious in most

parts of the world, and it usually carries hefty penalties with it. The same thing goes for recording someone's conversation without their permission. And no, their manager cannot consent on their behalf. So if your assessment has an objective such as "demonstrate access to mailbox", find another way to prove it than reading an actual email (compromise credentials, download PST-file, snapshot the Exchange server, etc.).

So, if you experience a client asking for something to be tested, or your sales representative has offered something that violates any of these, then it is, unfortunately, left to you to speak up and point out that these activities might violate your local laws, and ask that legal counsel be involved.

If the preceding makes perfect sense to you, then feel free to skip the rest of this chapter. Otherwise, the following are some practical examples of where laws specific to my region, but quite possibly relevant to yours too, might apply.

When can you test a web application?
The second we get permission by someone who owns the system. That means the application owner, or the owner's boss, or the boss's boss and so on. No one, not even the CEO of a company, can give you permission to test something that they don't own. This is why it's so important to spot whenever something looks like it integrates with 3rd parties. It's illegal to touch it, and the individual consultant risks going to prison. You want your client to contact those 3rd parties and obtain permission.

When can you test a mobile app?
It depends. The application itself, you can do that all day long, because as long as it's running on your device, you own the app instance. You might still violate End User License Agreements and Acceptable Use Policies, but that's a different matter and won't see you in prison.

But the second you start touching the APIs and backends, you need permission, because you are now interacting with someone else's system.

Does the application owner also own the server that it runs on?
No, they most likely don't, so they can't tell you that it's OK to try and break into the server that's running the application. This is why you always want to put both the application name/URL, and the IP/hostname in the Statement of Work and the scope, so that the owners of the whole thing, or someone with mandate to do so, gives you permission. This is also why, when you find a Remote Command Execution vulnerability, you should call the client and ask for permission to go beyond the server, before trying to do so.

This also applies if you crash the application. That's fine, you have permission to target it, but what if you crash the server? So this should be included in the permissions, or otherwise you should refrain from touching it.

Cost and responsibilities

I intentionally did not put this at the top of the chapter, as this should be the most obvious reason. One of the key outputs of a scoping session is of course the estimate of how much time is needed for the work, or the expected cost of the work. How to arrive at this estimate will be discussed in detail in chapter 6.

The secondary purpose is for the technical consultant to determine what pre-requisites and practicalities are needed to be able to perform the assessment in the estimated time. These will be discussed further in chapter 3, but this should not be limited to that which the client needs to provide, but likewise what the consultant needs to provide to the client (contact details, proof of vetting, etc.).

The output of the scoping session should also be that any constraints are known before the project starts, such as assets or features that cannot be touched for legal reasons, that aren't ready for testing yet, or items that the consultancy is not willing or able to assess due to lack of skills, personnel, time, etc.

Practicalities

The final reason for having a formal scoping session and resulting document, is a practical one. First of all, unless the consultancy is working project-to-project, there will likely be a planning and scheduling element involved. Having the scoping session means that the clients' deadlines and timetables can be taken into consideration, and the consultants' estimate is part of that. The scope and the identified pre-requisites also lets everyone involved know what needs to be done, by whom and by when, and the scheduling needs to allow for all of that.

Lastly, having written an effective Statement of Work, complete with context, purpose and approach, any consultant should be able to pick it up and appreciate the importance of the project, where it fits into the larger body of work being undertaken by the client, and how to provide the best value for the client in that context. These are the principles of *Believe* and *Decentralized Command* described in the book *Extreme Ownership* by Jocko Willink and Leif Babin, which I would highly recommend. The document likewise serves as a worksheet for people on both sides, in that it lets everyone know what needs to be covered and performed during the execution of the assessment.

3. What
What to include in a scope

You've had your meeting with the client, they told you everything and you understand exactly what needs to be done. What should you write in the Scope section of your proposal? Let's consider the example from our introductory chapter. To make the reading easier, the following pages have the content of our sample Statement of Work document on the left page, and the explanation and arguments for why it is so, on the right page.

Statement of Work

ACME is implementing the ABC product to monitor, deploy and manage the SSL/TLS certificates across the ACME environments. As such, ACME require assurances regarding the security posture of the ABC product and it's current implementation in the ACME test environment.

To provide this, ConsultingCompany will conduct a configuration review of the deployed solution thick client and a web application security assessment of its Internet-exposed web interface, based on available documentation and manual review of files accessible on the server installed and configured with the ABC product. Additionally, ConsultingCompany will investigate how the solution employs the ACME protocol for deploying certificates and ensure that this aligns with industry best practices and does not expose ACME to additional risks.

Your document's initial purpose may very well be to convince the client to contract with you or your company. However, once this is achieved, the document may very well serve a secondary purpose; explaining to your colleagues (or reminding yourself of) the context of the project and what work needs to be performed. For this reason alone, the introduction should explain in layman's terms what the target of your efforts will be, and the context in which that target is to be employed. You might think that simply describing it as a web application should be plenty of context, but the focus and impact of findings might very well differ vastly if the application is used by a financial institution (being subject to Anti-Money Laundering (AML) and financial regulations), a merchant or payment provider (being subject to the Payment Card Industry (PCI) compliance programme) or a gambling services provider (being subject to both, as well as gambling regulations and oversight). For instance, the lack of a visible clock on all pages of a web application will be of next-to-no importance for a financial institution, but it will be the difference between losing your license or not for gambling providers in certain regions.

Not only does this show your client that you understand their asset, the context in which it's deployed, and the industry in which they operate, it also gives the performing consultant a fair warning that these might be areas they need to read up on prior to the assessment start date.

If you are undertaking work that isn't part of your standardised services, this is also a good place to point out any custom work to be performed, again so you're showing this to the client early in the text while they're still focused, and giving your colleague a warning that this project is more than "just" the standard body of work.

The assessment will focus on the following:

- Determining the security posture of the Internet-exposed web interface by conducting a web application security assessment
- Identifying how the solution communicates with other assets as part of the certificate monitoring and deployment process
- Determining how the solution generates and stores certificates locally, along with its related secrets management

While it may be possible to infer it from the preceding text, it is well worth the effort to summarise the primary objectives of the engagement into a bullet-list of single paragraphs. These should reflect the main worries and concerns the client has expressed during your scoping session. This will help you ensure that your work, when performing the assessment, remains focused on answering these concerns and providing the value expected by the client. Providing these as a condensed bullet-list also makes it easier for the client to review and validate this focus, as lists (when not of excessive length) has a tendency to draw the eye of the reader.

If the client failed to present their concerns, or if the main stakeholders were not part of the session (not an uncommon occurrence), you may need to default to generic and fluffy objective statements such as "Determining the overall security posture of the solution, identify security issues that could present a risk to the client, ensure compliance with regulatory and company-stated baselines, and identify compensating controls and mitigation strategies to lower the risk to be within the risk appetite of the client". These will be discussed further in chapter 6.

Given that web applications are often the primary attack surface for organisations, it is crucial to prioritise their security in order to protect critical business assets. The objective of a web application security assessment is to ensure that the target application incorporates the necessary security controls and robust implementation to safeguard business assets, end users, and the organization's reputation.

A web application security review involves searching for design flaws, vulnerabilities, and inherent weaknesses in the design. This assessment involves analysing the functionality of the target application and attempting to use it in unintended ways that were not specified during the design process. Such unintended functionality may include unauthorised manipulation and viewing of data, as well as identifying programming or configuration errors.

The assessment activities focuses on these key areas:

- Open source information gathering
- Application reconnaissance and fingerprinting
- Configuration management
- Data and input validation
- Authentication and authorization model review
- Session management implementation
- Error handling and business logic
- Cryptography of data at rest and in transit
- Dynamic internet application functionalities

In particular, for this assessment the emphasis will be on determining the overall security posture of the application, uncover weaknesses and vulnerabilities that could present a risk to the client, ensure compliance with regulatory oversights and company stated baselines and identify compensating controls and suggested mitigation strategies to lower the risk to be within the risk appetite of the client. The final objective of the assessment will be to determine if the solution is fit for purpose, or can be made so with additional security hardening, to make it a viable component in ACME's production environment.

With the context and the objectives taken care of, now comes the time describe how you intend for the assessment to achieve those objectives. As in the example, the project may be aligned with a standard offering of the consultancy (lets face it, everyone probably has a standard description for how they approach web application security assessments), which describes the high-level methodology being used, standards being adhered to, pre-defined tasks and sub-components that make up the service, etc. But if you do not, then this is your chance to start building it. For many years I would reinvent the wheel, and write out the approach of the project by hand (which resulted in me more or less memorising the example, verbatim) so please endeavour to be smarter than me.

Describe the service, why such a service is needed, and what the overall, generic, approach to it is. This won't be covered in any more detail in this book, as this really should be part of your service and business development as a security consultancy person or company. But, at a high level it should contain the following:

- What the service is
- Why it is needed
- What work you will be doing as part of the service
- Key activities within that work, such as:
    - Attack surface discovery
    - Enumeration and reconnaissance
    - Payload development (whether that be XSS, SQLI or ROP-chains)
    - Exploitation and post-exploitation
- Any other checks you want to remind your consultant to do, and want to reassure your client that they will be done
- Alignment with testing standards, such as the OSSTM, PTES, OWASP SAMM or Testing Guide, etc.
- Alignment with reporting standards and vulnerability categorisation, such as OWASP Top 10, Biztec TEC 11, CWE Top 25, etc.

Whenever you find yourself writing one of these, please make sure to save a copy that is generic enough so as not to identify your client, and which can be reused as a starting point for the next time a similar project comes in for scoping. This may sound trivial, but over time, this will save you a surprising amount of effort.

Scope

The following components will be in scope for this assessment:

- server1.acme.com - 192.168.13.37
- server2.acme.com - 192.168.42.42
- https://ABC.acme.com

The XYZ feature of ABC accessible at https://ABC.acme.com/dangerousfeature has been deemed out of scope due to INSERT_VALID_REASON and will not be targeted during this assessment.

The assessment will be conducted as a grey-box assessment, as ConsultingCompany will be provided with valid user accounts and detailed system documentation

Now that we know what we're doing, why we're doing it and how we're doing, it's time to nail down what we're doing it to. As discussed in the introduction, this needs to include all hostnames, applications, IP addresses, etc. that are to be targeted during the assessment. It also needs to list any specific items or activities that will be left out of the assessment.

This section is also where you would put how much time the project is estimated to take (more on this in chapter 6.), and possibly the expected schedule of the project. This is primarily left to the discretion of your Sales representative and/or planning functions, and whether these be included or not is largely a matter of your local business practice.

The following pre-requisites must be delivered prior to the assessment start-date to ensure an effective assessment:

- Whitelisting/allowlisting in firewalls
- Application documentation, including documentation of authentication and authorization mechanisms, API methods, requests and responses with their expected parameters
- Data set that can be used with the target in the appropriate environment, such as client IDs, card numbers etc.
- Sufficiently long timeout value on any authorization token used for testing
- Architecture diagram of the solution
- Baselines employed on server1.acme.com and server2.acme.com
- Contact details of technical persons that can provide explanations on the workings of the application

Lastly, the pre-requisites. A lot of these will seem obvious to you, because you are the one with experience performing the work, but for your client they might not be so obvious. Remember, when you assume, you make an "ASS" of "U" and "Me". So spell it out, and don't assume that anyone really understands the work you're preparing for.
If you are assessing a web application, then obviously you will need to know the URL of the application, and if there's a login, you will most likely need credentials. But how many, and what type of credentials? Do you need multiple of each type? And what about the IP address of the server or servers hosting the application? Or the user guide, or installation guide, or maybe architecture diagrams that help you understand the flow of data. Or the secure configuration baseline used for that server, and the software development guidelines the developers used, or the Bill of Materials for any 3rd party components, a copy of their patch-management policy, data privacy policy, acceptable use policy, etc. Do you need specific firewall openings to be able to perform your test? Or how about a full development environment where you can build the custom product the client is asking you test?

Only you know what you really need to perform the best possible project, and it is in the clients' best interest to help you as much as possible to make the project a success, as that is the way they will ultimately achieve their objectives. So share the burden, explain to the client what you need and why, and most of them will be happy to help you.

Depending on the complexity of the project, and your existing familiarity with the client, a scope such as this may be considered overkill. For clients whom you've done plenty of work with in the past, it might be sufficient to simply put in five lines stating what will be done, and leave everything else to the discretion of the consultant. But this invites ambiguity, and it truly does not scale well. That approach will work when the person scoping and performing the assessment are the same, when the person requesting the project and supporting the execution of it are the same, etc. And it only works until a conflict arises.

The approach and pre-requisites are largely going to be consistent across most projects, so maintaining a polished library of these across your offering means those sections can be completed in a very short amount of time. The scope itself will be subject to change for every project, as the assets will be different, but surely inserting a few names and IP addresses is short work. That leaves the statement of work and the objectives, which should be born out of conversation with the client, and as such will (or at least should) be unique. This is where the effort comes in, but as you can see, the net result is that you really only need to write about 200 words of custom content to produce a superb document. We'll discuss in more depth how to do this in chapter 6.

4. Who

Division of labour, roles and responsibilities, who does what? In the larger context of proposal writing, the Sales representative is ultimately responsible for the document that goes out, as they are traditionally the ones submitting it to the client. This means that the final reading through, making sure that everything looks proper and polished ultimately rests on the Sales representative. The same applies for the initial value proposition, the section that convinces the client why they should enter into a deal with you.

The role of technical consultants is to be just that, technical. A good technical consultant is someone who is strong in the technical aspects of the work, but with a bit of business understanding. A strong Sales representative is someone with a strong business understanding, but with a bit of technical knowledge. Together, they make an unstoppable team. Sales will likely have a broader view of the company, and can better speak to all the qualities that make them a good fit for the customer, but they can always do with input from the consultant to really make the value proposition shine. And for some, it might also be prudent to have them review such a proposition to ensure that nothing is overstated or that checks aren't being written that the consultant can't cash.

Inversely, the Statement of Work and the Scope are items that are (likely) best understood by the consultant, and as such the full responsibility of writing this should rest on the consultant. That is not to say the Sales representative should not read through it, ensuring that the context and business objectives have been correctly understood by both (if each of you have opposing understandings of what the client asked for, more likely than not one of you is wrong). This is also to ensure that the quality of writing aligns with the rest of the document. Any complaints coming back from the client regarding the proposal document should under no circumstances be met with "oh, a consultant wrote that, it wasn't me!" or "that's just something Sales put in, it's not actually what we do", because to be honest, the client doesn't care. All they know is that the company sent a document, the figurehead of the company is YOU (whether you're in Sales or a consultant), so they will direct any grievances to YOU. So if you find yourself being the one sending the proposal, make sure to read it and that you are happy with both the content and the presentation of it.

A word on Quality Assurance

Should proposals, statements of work and scopes go through a Quality Assurance (QA) process? The short answer; yes! The better answer; it depends. Assuming you have a high-performing team, where each part takes ownership of the ultimate product, then a QA process should not be necessary. Each party will naturally read through the entire document, suggest changes, and the team will ensure that the document shines. A consultant might briefly pass the statement of work, scope and pre-requisites around to colleagues for a sanity check, Sales will have a well-rehearsed value proposition that can quickly be aligned to the client with the combined efforts of the department, and the output will be a finalised and polished product.

But in the rare case where this is not the way your team performs, who should perform the QA? Surely a consultant won't have the business understanding to critique the value proposition, and only a consultant could truly appreciate and point out flaws in the statement of work, right? Wrong! If this was true, then that would mean that 90% of your document would be impossible for the client to understand, because they will be in neither of those roles. In fact, nearly anyone with an eye for detail should be able to QA the full document, based on the basic tenant that if a "normal" person is unable to understand your proposition, descriptions and scope, then neither will your customer.

5. When

So when should you write a formal proposal, Statement of Work and Scope, and when can you make do with a simple email? Well, as with the legal aspects, this will vary depending on where you operate. In all regions where I have worked, an agreement over e-mail is just as legally binding as a signed piece of paper, so I would say it depends on how much description is needed to understand the work to be undertaken.

"Can you please have a look at XYZ and write a one-page statement about how effective it is compared to ABC?" - This would be an example of a task that I would happily manage over e-mail. The objective is clear-cut, and the implication is that you have free range to determine how to best compare the two items. Pre-requisites would likewise be straight-forward, you would need a copy of XYZ and ABC, and you'd be ready to start.

When dealing with anything more complex than that, I would always prefer proper documentation, as it will always be easier to go back through and point to and say "this is what we agreed upon", rather than flipping through multiple e-mail threads that may or may not have been thoroughly read by everyone involved.

So how soon should you start writing your Statement of Work and Scope? Well, assuming you are as busy in your work as I have always been, there's no time like the present. I advocate for writing these things while the scoping session is ongoing, at least in a first rough draft version. This way you can sanity-check everything with the client before the session ends, and you won't have to waste time sending a document with misunderstandings in it, only to then have to redo the work. The second-best option is to write it immediately after the session, while everything is still fresh in your memory. Remember, unless it is a unique, insanely custom project, your effort will predominantly be spent on writing 200 words and picking the right building blocks from your library as discussed in chapter 3.

Also in the category of "when", although not strictly part of the scoping process but rather that of scheduling a project and estimate the effort, I want to share with you my thoughts on assigning multiple consultants to a single project for the purpose of meeting clients' deadlines and completing a project faster. This is the kind of logic that only works if you believe nine women to be able to give birth to a baby in one month.

A consultant will often spend half to a whole day getting set up for a project and familiarising themselves with their target. This is not something that can be parallelised, as each consultant will need to go through this on their own regardless. Merging the findings of someone else with your own report also produces overhead, and can add anywhere from a couple of hours to half a day to your efforts. Now multiply that by the number of consultants you have assigned to the project. You also have to assume a 20% overlap in testing, simply due to everyone's need to understand the target and shared responsibilities in the features and functionality of a target.

Take these numbers and add in your own experience, and you should be able to calculate the minimum size of a project before it makes sense to attempt to parallelise it, or determine how many days need to be added to your estimate. There's a balancing act in finding out how many consultants can be added before the overhead actually means the project will finish later as opposed to sooner due to more resources being thrown at it.

In the same vein, if you decide to split a project into multiple sub-projects, expect the same overhead. For this reason, you should never split projects unless there's a natural split, and each sub-component can be completed in isolation so as to not add extra work in merging the parts into a whole.

Let's try and do the math on this.

To calculate the maximum number of consultants n that can be added to a project of duration X, before the overhead exceeds the project duration, we need to consider the following factors:

1. Setup and familiarization time per consultant: S (in days or hours), taken by each consultant.

2. Merging overhead per consultant: M (in days or hours), as every additional consultant's work needs to be integrated with the others.

3. Testing overlap (20% of total testing time): This scales with the number of consultants *n*.

The formula for calculating the overhead becomes:

$$\text{Overhead} = S \times n + M \times (n - 1) + 0.2 \times n \times X$$

This overhead must not exceed *X*, the total project duration. Therefore, the inequality is:

$$S \times n + M \times (n - 1) + 0.2 \times n \times X \leq X$$

This can be simplified and re-arranged into:

$$(S + M + 0.2 \times X) \times n - M \leq X$$

Lastly, you can solve for *n*, which gives us the following formula:

$$n_{max} = \left\lfloor \frac{X + M}{S + M + 0.2 \times X} \right\rfloor$$

Here, the floor function ensures *n* is an integer, as you can't have fractional consultants.

Using this, you'll find that you can have up to two consultants on a five-day project without the overhead exceeding the project duration. But if you have three consultants, then you need at least 10 days, and for four consultants you need a staggering 30 days. But keep in mind, this is without considering how much time is ACTUALLY left for unique work. In the 5-day example, 4.5 days will be spent on the overhead or duplicate work.

While the math here may be crude (I'm not a mathematician) it should help push the idea that you want to be mindful of how you staff and split a project, and when you do split it, that you make the effort to split it in a way that avoids overlap, as that is really the factor that eats away at the numbers.

6. How
How to do everything from the previous chapters

So now, with all the background and context out of the way, let's get to the core of this subject. How do you scope a security assessment?

Scoping nearly always starts with you receiving some information about the client and what it is they want or need. This can be in the form of someone simply telling you what desires the client has expressed, it can be an email with some rough ideas and documentation about a thing that they want tested, or it can be a more formal test request or request for proposals.

If you are dealing with a client who has a lot of experience with procuring security assessments, the material they forward you may in fact be all the information you need, and this is thankfully something that is becoming more common. If that is the case, then you've already read everything you need (except maybe the art of estimating your work) and can get started writing. In most instances, however, the brief is just that; brief, and you will need to have a scoping meeting or call with the client to fully understand and appreciate what it is they're after.

How to run a scoping meeting
In my experience, the client will most often be the one inviting for the scoping meeting, and if that is the case, you have very little to do other than to show up on the day with everything they've provided up front read, your most constructive and curious mindset, and a list of intelligent questions to uncover the project details. However, if you ever get the chance to organise a scoping session, or if the session planned by the client ends up lacking forward momentum (as in no one on the call really knows what to do or how to run the meeting) here is a list of steps and activities you should strive to get through during the meeting.

The invite

When inviting for a scoping meeting, or really any meeting regardless of the topic, make sure to always include an agenda. In a corporate setting, it is almost universally accepted that there are too many meetings, so you want to make sure that your meeting gets priority and that participants are as well-prepared as possible, and an agenda is a great tool for that. The following is a proposed agenda for a generic scoping meeting, along with the rational for each:

Introductions and roles	Going around the room and having everyone introduce themselves, simply stating their name, title and role, is a tried and tested Sales stable. While traditionally people in sales roles might have done this to get a chance to write down what contacts are in a meeting and who to follow up with, it actually serves a much bigger purpose. The simple act of saying something, anything, and being given the time and opportunity to do so in a group setting, makes you more likely to speak up if you see or hear a mistake about to be made, and generally enforces the idea that it is OK for everyone to participate in the conversation. This might seem odd and out of place, but regardless of how you feel about it in the moment, it still works. And it works in multiple settings. While this knowledge originates from a 1990 cockpit resource management in the aviation industry[1], in 2006 Dr. Martin A. Makary and his team at Johns Hopkins applied the same to improve teamwork in surgical teams.[2]

---

[1] Helmreich RL, Wilhelm JA, Gregorich SE, Chidester TR. Preliminary results from the evaluation of cockpit resource management training: performance ratings of flightcrews. Aviat SpaceEnviron Med 1990;61:576–579

[2] https://www.researchgate.net/publication/7133335_Operating_Room_Teamwork_among_Physicians_and_Nurses#read

Background and context

Everyone is busy, and a lot of the time, people accept meeting invites without reading any of the invite or being told about the purpose up front.

So it is worth spending two minutes explaining the purpose of the meeting, how it is to get an understanding of WHAT is to be assessed, WHY it needs to be assessed, and why the people in the meeting have been invited.

Context, as they say, is king, and when it comes to identifying security issues in a product or process, it pays great dividend to understand in what context the product or process is to be used, and why it was created in the first place.

Not only does this give you insights into the timeframe within which the asset was implemented (did they rush it and skip security requirements, or did they take their time?) it also lets you better frame any potential findings you might have after the assessment is over, and better and more accurately describe the impact of your findings.

Knowing the context in which something is to be used, may also be the difference between only finding a few low-risk technical issues, and finding a few low-risk technical issues and an earth-shattering critical procedural vulnerability that was overlooked by all the technical people implementing this thing.

Previous work and demonstrations

If the client doesn't offer up this information on their own, ask!

Ask what work has previously been done to determine the security posture of the asset that you will be investigating, what the results were, and what issues have been resolved.

This will give you an indication of the current state of the asset, and inform your decisions of how much time to spend looking for specific vulnerability categories.

For instance, did the previous assessment identify buffer overflow vulnerabilities so they re-wrote the whole thing in a memory-safe language? If so, then there will be little point looking for that now.

Or did they implement input validation using a specific framework to avoid Cross-Site Scripting vulnerabilities? If so, you might need to spend extra time looking into how to circumvent or test that framework, rather than targeting all input in the actual application. And so on.

Also ask the client to demonstrate the thing they want tested. When technical staff is asked to present something that they implemented, during a meeting with their supervisors or managers, they are essentially put on the spot and may feel like they are being indirectly asked to justify their existence within the company.

For this reason the descriptions may become exceedingly complicated and convoluted, when the assessment target to you might actually seem really simple.

For this reason, it is often preferable to ask for a basic demonstration of the expected use cases and feature sets, so you get a rough idea of the attack surface and number of features you will be targeting in your assessment.

Questions and pre-mortem

Even after being presented with the background, the context, and the demonstration, you might still have questions. Or the client might have questions for you, about how the project is to be performed.

Make sure to set aside ample time for such questions, as they will almost certainly make or break the project.

We will discuss a few such questions and the concept of "pre-mortem" in the next section, which is how you can bring your and their collective experiences to bear to ensure a smoother project.

Planning

While it may seem trivial, something as practical as "when do you need it?" and "when can you start?" should always be part of the discussion. This should also include physical conditions, such as whether or not a project can be performed remotely, needs to be onsite, require specific language skills, clearances, interacting with different time zones, working odd hours, etc.

The meeting

Ultimately, your goal for the meeting is to identify the needs and wants of the client, align that with the type of consultancy you whish to deliver and your capabilities, estimate and plan the work, and win the project. Following the agenda just described should get you a large part of the way there. Being clear about why you're there (to help!), honest about what you can and cannot do, and asking open-ended questions should get you the rest of the way. Always assume that no one in the meeting really knows why they're there (it happens more often than you'd think) and you can only get positively surprised. At the same time, you will already be in the explanatory mindset and mentally prepared to explain how and why things need to happen in a certain way. Explain to the participants, or have the client contact explain, that an assets needs to undergo an assessment to determine it's current security posture, and that you (if you get the project) are there to help validate all the good work they've done in securing the asset and ensure that no evil hackers will, well, hack it. Emphasis should be put on the fact that it is not a "you VS them" scenario

Language

Roles

Generally speaking, consulting falls into three distinct categories:

- Subject Matter Experts (SME)
- Collaborators
- Extra set of hands

The "Extra set of hands" is essentially untrained hired help, staff augmentation, student workers and similar. For these, a very clear and descriptive task exists, and the client simply wants you to get it done in accordance with that description because they themselves don't have the time. This is generally not the role in which we work, or event want to work.

The Collaborators are when consultants take on the role of a sparring partner, or a coach, where the objective is to highlight possible solutions together. In this, the client and you are equal, and both bring knowledge and experience to the table. This is a common area for us to work in when dealing with Governance and Risk Management, or when discussing larger security improvement or testing programmes with clients.

Lastly, the SME, which is where the vast majority of our work usually lies. This role is for the type of work that involves technical questions, fact-finding missions, require specialist know-how. These are essentially when the client team doesn't have enough knowledge and wishes to retain outside help to answer questions ("is this vulnerable?") or help make decisions for them.

Your role as a consultant affects the language you use, and lack of experience, differences in age, or perceived authority when faced with senior executives or representatives from big impressive corporate entities, may cause you to become overly submissive, confrontational, or maybe overconfident. So recognizing your role, and being clear about what role you intend to enter on the given project, helps align the language between you and the client team. If you whish to learn more about the respective roles, and consulting in general, I would highly recommend Peter Block's *Flawless Consulting*, but for now, this rough categorization will be sufficient.

Body language and presentation

While body language can be an entire study onto itself (and I would very much recommend *What Every Body Is Saying* by Joe Navarro and Marvin Karlins for those interested), rather than putting much initial stock in the body language of the client participating in the meeting, I want to focus on a few areas relating to yourself.

Confidence is attractive. Overconfidence is not. Projecting confidence does not mean you have it, and even if you're not projecting confidence, you might still have it. We generally want the client to have confidence in our abilities, and this starts with us presenting ourselves as confident. The easiest way to do this (and your parents might very well have told you this) is; to sit up straight, and make yourself presentable. The second way is by invoking a sense of isopraxism.

> Isopraxism is a neurobehavior that humans display in which we copy each other in order to make both parties feel safe, and it's part of the process of developing rapport which leads to trust. While this is normally something that is done unconsciously, via speech patterns, body language, tempo, etc., it can actively be done via vocabulary as well. This is also commonly referred to as "mirroring". It can also be done through something as simple as clothing. So it is worth having a quick search online for pictures from the company you're meeting with, to get an indication of what the formal or informal dress-code is, and mimic it as much as you are able or willing to. Does this mean you should wear a suit and tie, even though you are a baggy-jeans-and-hoodie kinda person? No, absolutely not. But it does mean you might want to consider dressing up just a little, or down if the opposite happens to be the case. It also means you should try and use the same vocabulary as your client, which of course gets easier the more you work with them. While you might have very strong opinions about what is and isn't a "pentest", if that's the term the client uses, you are probably better of adopting that same term when dealing with this client. If they gesticulate a lot when they talk, see if you can do the same (but make sure it doesn't look like you're imitating them). At its root, this biological principal is very simple; we fear what is different, and we are drawn to that which is similar, it makes us feel safe, and feeling safe is good. If you can make me feel safe, I am much more likely to trust you, and have confidence in what you're saying.

Lastly, a word about your size. I am not a small person, I am above-average in both height and weight, and for some reason I have an unconscious tendency to "occupy" or "take over" a room when I enter. This in the past made me a very dominating figure in any meeting, to the extent that it would intimidate meeting participants that didn't know me (I'm really super friendly, I promise), which meant they would be hesitant to speak up. A simple, yet effective, solution to this was shared with me by a fellow giant (and my mentor); duck your head when entering the room, and place your hands under the table. It seems so simple, yet the effect was immediate. Obviously ducking your head removes a tiny bit of your height, but it also adds a tiny bit of submissiveness to your physical profile. Placing your hands under the table, likewise reduces your stature, which again makes you seem less imposing.

Of course, the inverse also applies. If you are short or lite, raise your head, and fold your hands on the table, as this will increase your overall physical presence. This can likewise be used actively, to either invite inquiry (place your hands under the table, lower your head) or underline a statement (place your hands on the table and hold your head up). While I make no claim to fully understand the mechanisms that make this work, personal experience and that of those I've taught, shows that this can make a significant difference, so it's worth trying out.

Language and getting people to talk
Being aware of your own presence in the room (and yes, this also applies to online meetings) and with isopraxism invoked through all the physical means, it's time to get people talking. The obvious way is to follow the outline of the agenda, but if you really want them to spill it, try to put on an act of Echoism.

> The concept of echoism was introduced by Dr. Craig Malkin in his book *Rethinking Narcissism*, which is a highly recommended read. It serves as a counterpart to narcissism and describes a pattern of relating to others, in which the subject exhibits a self-effacing or self-sacrificing orientation towards others, while narcissism involves an excessive focus on oneself and a need for admiration.
>
> Echoists are often highly empathetic and sensitive to the emotions and needs of others. They possess a genuine ability to understand and connect with others on an emotional level. This empathy can be a valuable quality in relationships, allowing them to provide support, comfort, and understanding to those around them.

Emulating this gives ample room and opportunity for the people around you to share their thoughts, and for any narcissists (managers and technical experts often exist quite high on the narcissistic spectrum) it will "lure" them into filling that room with details of the current topic (the assessment we're currently trying to scope).

Echoists also tend to prioritize harmony and avoid conflict. They strive to maintain peaceful and cooperative relationships with others. Their accommodating nature can contribute to smoother interactions and a more amicable environment, fostering positive and harmonious connections with others, which, as it turns out, is exactly the atmosphere we want in most meetings. Echoists also excel at listening to others and validating their experiences. They are attentive and responsive to the feelings and concerns of those around them. Their ability to provide a safe space for others to express themselves and feel understood can foster deeper connections and strengthen relationships, which, again, is very conducive in most meetings, and tie into labelling (which we'll get to shortly).

So how do you actively adopt these echoist traits, if that is not who you are naturally?

- Practice Active Listening: Engage in active listening by giving your full attention to others when they speak. Focus on understanding their perspective, feelings, and needs without interrupting or immediately shifting the conversation to yourself or your own company. Show empathy and validate their experiences (labelling, we'll get to it soon, I promise).
- Cultivate Empathy: Develop your empathetic skills by putting yourself in others' shoes and seeking to understand their emotions and experiences. This will help you connect with others on a deeper level and respond to their needs with genuine care and understanding. Even though this is business, make no mistake, there are a lot of feelings and emotions tied up in peoples work.
- Set Healthy Boundaries: While it's important to be accommodating, remember to establish and communicate your own (and your consultancy's) boundaries. Learn to say no when necessary (the project is outside of your capabilities or company interests).
- Be quiet. Most people become uncomfortable after about four seconds of silence, and will often offer up more details on the subject or their thoughts on the matter if you are simply silent.

You can combine isopraxism and echoism to great effect. One of the most effective combinations is alarmingly simple; mirror what was just said, in the same way that it was said (or go up on the last syllable), and be silent for four seconds. Let's imagine that your client just told you "Your estimate is too high". That's not a very informative thing to say, as it provides you with nothing to retort with other than "no it isn't", which is unlikely to get you very far. But, if you simply reply "too high?" and wait for a few seconds in silence, the social pressure and discomfort will almost always cause them to detail and attempt to justify their answer, which provides you with a plethora of information, and possible something you can use to produce a better answer, or find a way to adjust your estimate to their liking.

For a more detailed examination of the two concepts, I would recommend Craig Malkin's *Rethinking Narcissism*, and Chriss Voss' *Never Split The Difference*.

Scoping questions

One of the most important things to uncover during a scoping session, is the need of the client. Notice that I write "need", while in the beginning of this chapter we also discussed the clients "wants". Those two might not necessarily be the same, and in fact it is quite common for the two to differ. This is why you want your line of questioning to lead to the "need" so you can validate their "wants" and propose the right body of work.

As we discussed in The statement of work, our line of questioning must lead us to an understanding of the thing that we are to assess, why it needs to be assessed, what client questions our work is to help answer, and against what threats and risks it needs to be evaluated. This is so that we can recommend the right type of assessment, describe this to our future self or a colleague who will perform the work but weren't involved in the scoping, and accurately estimate the work.

The following questioning framework has served me well, so I share it here with you, hoping that it will do the same for you.

1. **In simple terms, what is it?** - It's hard to know what to do, if you don't know what you're doing it to. So this is always my first question. I usually exaggerate the question by asking "is it a car, a ship, a web application, smartphone app, what?"
2. **In layman's terms, what is it used for?** - Explain it to me like I'm five. If the answer to the previous question was overly convoluted, this will usually bring it into the realm of normal understanding, and you will already at this point start to develop an idea of what type of work needs to go into testing it. Examples of answers would be "it's for online banking, you can do transactions and view accounts and such" or "it's for booking appointments" or "it downloads and analyses the data" etc.
3. **In technical terms, what does it do?** - What technology is used, what it is built on, what programming language, operating system, frameworks, etc. These are all things that might not be super important to estimate the work, but it's information that is useful when deciding on which consultant to put on the project (someone with experience in these things) or what technology you might need to read up on prior to, and it also presents the client with an opportunity to demonstrate their knowledge and experience with the technology, which plays well into our previous topic of Echoism. This is also the part where you can ask them to show you architecture drawings, system sequence diagrams, process flowcharts, mock-ups, screenshots, etc.
4. **In business terms, why did you build/buy/implement it?** - Knowing what

problem it is they are trying to solve with this, gives you a blueprint for what it is, as an offensive operator, you are trying to disrupt, and by extension better informs you to determine the impact of technical and logical findings you might make during the assessment.

5. **Who are the intended users of it?** - Knowing if the users will be ultra-tech-savvy (and therefore less likely to fall for phishing and similar manipulative attacks) or if it will be less aware "normal" users, relates to the likelihood of exploitation of your to-be-identified vulnerabilities. Knowing if there will be different user roles (guest, user, administrator, supervisor, etc.) informs whether you will need to repeat the same testing multiple times in different contexts, or if you should expect to do additional work with regards to authentication and authorization controls.

6. **How will the end-user use it?** - This is important, because this will in most cases be your primary attack surface, in effect the way or vector with which you will be doing most of your testing. Is it something in a browser? Is it server-to-server through a web-service (is it SOAP, REST, or a binary protocol?), or an application using an API?

7. **What is required to interact with it, and is anything off-limits?** - Will you need a username and password, a client certificate, your IP allow-listed, do you need a special client or software, specific originating IP address, etc. These are things you don't want to wait to find out about on the day of the test. If there are specific features or assets that you are not allowed to interact with (mission-critical, likely to incur high costs, not owned by the client, etc.), this is also something you want to know and make sure to state very clearly in your scope.

8. **How many are there?** - Sometimes clients will present just a single instance, when in fact there are multiple, and while they might not say so, they could very well have an expectancy that you will be testing all of them. So it's better to ask. If it turns out that they have 50 assets that they want tested, and you estimate that testing one will take 10 days, they are unlikely to want to pay for 500 days in total, and to be honest, you are unlikely to WANT to spend 500 days testing those things. In these instances, consider and discuss with the client how different the instances are. Is it feasible to only test representative instances (one of each type), reducing the amount of work (and cost) and limiting the amount of mindless repetitive work?

9. **Has it been tested before?** - If it has, what were the findings, and have they been resolved? Where there's one flaw, there is usually more, so plan and expect to be spending time looking for the same type of vulnerabilities that were previously found, or at the very least spend some dedicated time testing if the remediation activities have in fact solved the problems and have not

introduced new ones.

10. **Why do you want it tested?** - If the client can't articulate what it is they wish to get out of this exercise, then no matter what you do and find, the project will be a failure and the client will end up either unhappy or disappointed. Don't be afraid to ask this question openly. Either the answer will be perfectly clear to the participants, and they will have no problem explaining to you why that is. Or it might be completely unknown to them, in which case it immediately highlights the need for additional information in order to ensure a successful project. It is extremely difficult to execute a successful project to completion, if the completion criteria are unknown. If they respond with "To make it secure" or "to be certain it's secure", then this is almost universally the wrong answer, and covers for the fact that the real reason is unknown to the participants. The "real" reasons for having a security assessment done, normally fall into one or more of these categories:
    a. Compliance reasons, as part of regulatory oversight and compliance frameworks or legal obligations
    b. It is part of a standard process that needs to be followed
    c. The client fears exploitation or abuse based on historical cases or current media focus on similar cases
    d. To answer specific questions or concerns ("is it possible to bypass XYZ" or "does ABC prevent XYZ"). If this is the case, get those specific questions and concerns and add them as the formal objectives of the project. This will also make reporting much easier, as these will be the core issues that your testing efforts must answer. You are essentially asking "what is your main concern about this, when you go to sleep at night?" and "what is making you feel this way?".

If you need more information on any one of the answers, remember what we discussed in Language and getting people to talk and simply mirror the last part of their answer, then remain silent. They will automatically elaborate on the topic, explain it in a different way, or give you examples that help fill out the gaps you're having.

After working through this line of questioning, you should have a pretty good idea about what it is you will be assessing, and you should be able to formulate a plan for how to execute the assessment. At this point you should also have an idea about what pre-requisites you will need in order to perform the assessment, all of which will later feed into estimating the effort required.

But what if what you're being asked to scope, is something you don't know anything about? Well, that's actually less of a problem than you might think. Obviously, it is preferable that you are well-versed in the subject matter, but for a lot of things it is actually very possible to both scope, estimate, and execute an assessment provided that you have an understanding of the general security concepts and security testing methodologies. Of course you will need to read up on the technology and experiment with it before the day of the assessment, and spar with colleagues who might have the needed experience (if they themselves can't be put on the project), but provided that you are honest with the client, and you can agree on what the body of work and objectives should look like, genuine value can be provided (and fantastic consulting and testing experience gained) on assessments of assets you have no prior experience with.

And what about nerves? Early on (and maybe even later on) you might find it very nerve-wreaking to be put in front of all these technical experts and be expected to figure out how to scope, estimate and execute a project. I think that is perfectly normal. You're being put on the spot and there's a bunch of people looking at you. And the worst part is, you have no idea what they're going to ask you. I think that's the unsettling part, because it makes it very hard to prepare for the situation. But the inverse is also true; THEY don't know what YOU'RE going to ask, so they're likely just as unsettled. So approach it like a human being, know what you know, and admit what you don't know. Then let them know that you'll go and find out. The more you do it, to less stressful that part becomes, and the more honest you are about it, the more confidence and trust the client will usually place in you.

For more inspiration on interview and questioning techniques, I would highly recommend the previously-mentioned book, *Never Split The Difference* by Chriss Voss, as well as *Bargaining with the Devil* by Rober Mnookin, and always strive to use open-ended questions.

> An open-ended question is a type of question that cannot be answered with a simple "yes" or "no" response. Instead, it encourages the person to provide more detailed and thoughtful answers, typically fostering a more extended and comprehensive conversation. Open-ended questions often begin with words like "how," "what," "why," or "tell me about," allowing the respondent to express their opinions, feelings, or experiences.
>
> For example, a closed-ended question could be "Is your security good?" Whereas an open-ended question would take the form of "What do you think about your current security controls? Can you share some specific mechanisms or challenges that stand out to you as critical?"

> This is why open-ended questions are commonly used in interviews, surveys, counselling sessions, and various communication contexts where the goal is to gather detailed information or encourage deeper discussions.

Dealing with hostility

In this line of work, it is unfortunately nearly inevitable that you will eventually run into individuals who exhibit general hostility towards your work. This is nothing personal. The thing to keep in mind, is that our job essentially exists because the quality of what someone else has done, is being brought into question. This might be triggered by compliance requirements (which means the regulatory body is questioning the quality), or it could be company policies (which means it's the company who's questioning it) or it might be a customer who's purchasing your products and services (in which case they are the ones questioning the quality). And that's not a very pleasant thing to realize, even if these doubts are often founded in historical examples that proved them right to be doubtful, and aren't tied directly to the person sitting in front of you in the meeting. This also often means that the person sitting in front of you in the meeting (physically or virtually) might not want to be in the meeting, or doesn't agree with the need for your services.

The regulatory body isn't present, the customer isn't either, and the company is the entity that the employee has been taught to be loyal towards. That unfortunately leaves only you for them to take their frustrations out on.

This is where labelling comes in, and it's a great tool for diffusing such a situation. However, sometimes we might know that this will be an issue, even before we start the meeting. In such instances, we can use something called an accusation audit, to get out in front of such hostility. For a more detailed discussion on both of these, I would again highly recommend Chriss Voss' *Never Split The Difference*, but I'll give you the highlights here:

> An accusation audit is a negotiation technique used to proactively address potential negative perceptions or objections the other party may have about you, your position, or the meeting itself. This approach disarms the other party, builds trust, and prepares the conversation for a more constructive dialogue.
>
> **Why we do it**
>
> 1. Neutralizes negative emotions: By acknowledging potential objections upfront, you remove their power and reduce the emotional charge they may carry.

2. Builds trust and transparency: It demonstrates honesty and self-awareness, which can make the other party more receptive and open.

3. Prevents surprises: Addressing potential issues before they are brought up avoids being blindsided during the negotiation and shows that you are prepared and considerate.

How to do it

1. Anticipate negatives: Before entering the negotiation, list all the potential objections, concerns, or negative thoughts the other party might have about you, your offer, or the situation.

2. Acknowledge the negatives: Begin by openly addressing these concerns in a non-defensive manner. Use phrases like:

- "You probably think…"
- "I know it might seem like…"
- "It's likely you're feeling…"

3. State the objections clearly: Mention each potential objection without trying to justify or explain it away. For example:

- "You probably think we're only interested in getting the biggest possible project"
- "I know it might seem like we haven't considered your constraints."
- "It's likely you're feeling like we don't understand your business"

4. Pause and allow response: After conducting the accusation audit, pause to give the other party a chance to confirm, deny, or discuss these concerns.

5. Avoid defensiveness: Your tone should be calm and understanding, not defensive or apologetic. This shows that you are empathetic and in control of the conversation.

An accusation audit helps pre-emptively diffuse potential friction, making it easier to move toward a mutually beneficial outcome in the meeting.

If you are blindsided by the hostility, you might not be able to perform an accusation audit (although if you can, great!) but you might be able to recover with labelling, and get the meeting back on track.

> Labelling is a negotiation technique used to acknowledge and validate the other party's emotions by identifying and naming them. It helps build rapport, defuse tension, and guide the conversation toward a positive outcome.
>
> **Why we do it**
>
> 1. Establishes empathy: Labelling shows that you are actively listening and understanding the other person's perspective, which builds trust and connection.
>
> 2. Defuses negative emotions: By naming emotions, you can address and reduce their intensity, making the other party feel heard and understood.
>
> 3. Gains control of the conversation: It subtly shifts the dialogue in a direction that acknowledges the other person's feelings without agreeing or disagreeing, allowing you to steer the negotiation more effectively.
>
> **How to do it**
>
> 1. Identify Emotions: Pay close attention to verbal and nonverbal cues, such as tone of voice, body language, and word choice, to sense what the other person is feeling.
>
> 2. Use Neutral Phrases: Start your label with phrases like:
>
> - "It seems like…"
> - "It sounds like…"
> - "It looks like…"
>
> 3. Name the emotion: Based on your observations, suggest what the other person might be feeling. For example:
>
> - "It seems like you're frustrated with the current situation."
> - "It sounds like you're worried about the timeline."
>
> 4. Pause and listen: After labelling, pause and give the other person time to respond. This allows them to clarify, correct, or expand on their feelings.
>
> 5. Avoid over-labelling: Be careful not to overuse labelling or sound condescending; it should feel natural and genuinely empathetic.

> Labelling helps you connect on an emotional level, leading to more productive interactions and outcomes.

Once you've labelled the situation, change the narrative of the meeting. Re-frame the purpose of conducting your security assessment from being about finding vulnerabilities, mistakes and misconfigurations, to being about validating and verifying all the good work that the client team has done. Everyone likes to feel validated, and by phrasing it like this you can subconsciously make the meeting about making the person opposite you look good. This will often change the dynamic of the meeting, and the participants will often start to open up more about the solution you are scoping, because they now feel like they are "showing off" all their good work. This in turn gives you an immense level of detail about the scope of your assessment, and may also gain you an ally during the assessment, in the form of the once-hostile meeting participant.

Ultimately, hostility should not be tolerated, it's unprofessional, and everyone deserves to be treated proper and with respect. But it might not be about you. In fact it almost never is. But if empathy, labelling, and re-framing the conversation fails to de-escalate the situation, do not be afraid to end the meeting. Especially if abusive language starts to be involved. In such instances, escalate to your seniors, reach out to your peers, or simply let the situation sit for a day, before returning to the client with another attempt or deciding to completely drop the engagement.

Ending the meeting

Once all parties are satisfied that they understand and agree on the contents and approach of the project, it's time to wrap it up. At this point in time, you should have a pretty good idea of whether or not you or your colleagues have the knowledge and skills to provide value to the project, or if the expectations and body of work is too far out of your reach for it to be conscionable to accept the project. While it might not be OK to tell the client to their face that you can't do the project (your company after all still wants to look good for the client, but policies on this will differ from company to company), it should ALWAYS be OK for you to tell your manager, sales, colleague, or if its your place, client, that you don't feel that you can in good-faith take on the project.

But, let's for a moment assume that you've decided that the project is a good fit for you and your company, and it's time to wrap up the meeting. When ending the meeting, do your best to label and mirror the concerns and descriptions of the project, to demonstrate your active listening. Retell the whole thing, the reason for the project and the scope of it, in your own words. Do your best to summarise the objectives that either the client has expressed, or what you feel would make for good objectives, and repeat the approach you which to take in seeking to meet those objectives. This gives the client a chance to confirm that your understanding is correct, that nothing has been missed from the scope, and that they agree or accept the proposed objectives and approach. This also gives them the opportunity to say "no, actually that's not right" after which they will be ready to tell you the correct version. That way you don't end up spending time writing up a statement of work that misses the mark.

Estimating and planning

Coming out of the meeting, you now have a fair idea about what it is that needs to be tested and why, and hopefully you have an idea about what type of standard service offering or bespoke body of work needs to be performed to achieve the clients' objectives. Now it's time to estimate the work.

In *Moonwalking with Einstein*, Joshua Foer uses the example of *chicken sexing* to illustrate a form of learning known as *subconscious or tacit knowledge*—knowledge that people acquire through experience and repetition, but can't necessarily explain. Chicken sexing is the process of determining the gender of baby chicks, which is important for the poultry industry. The task is incredibly difficult because male and female chicks look almost identical. Yet, experienced chicken sexers, after enough exposure, become extremely accurate at identifying the gender in just a second or two. They do this without being able to articulate exactly _how_ they know. This ability comes from a lot of practice and exposure, where their brains learn to recognize subtle, almost imperceptible differences. Foer uses this example to explain the concept of *implicit learning*—a type of learning where people become skilled at something through practice without necessarily forming a conscious, step-by-step understanding of the process. This contrasts with more explicit forms of knowledge, where learners can explain the logic behind their actions. Tacit knowledge and implicit learning is the standard approach to scoping most things as a security consultant, but as mentioned in the introduction, this creates a "chicken and egg" problem. So while the goal should be to arrive at this level via implicit learning, let's explore some alternative approaches that can be used prior to or while you are building up that body of exposure.

Calculus and scoping models

When exploring different scoping and project models, and most certainly when trying to estimate the effort required to complete the work, there are a few things that you should always keep in mind:

- Who can do the work?
    - What level of seniority or experience is required?
    - Does it require specific knowledge or language skills?
    - Does it require a security clearance, meaning that you might not be able to put your most experienced consultant or your subject matter expert on the project?
- Can the work be split into logical sub-components?
    - Can the work be parallelized?
    - Does it make sense to assign multiple people to the project?
    - Do you have multiple consultants available?

- - Keep in mind what we discussed in chapter 5 about overhead
- Are you the fastest or the slowest consultant you have?

If you are the fastest or most experienced consultant in your organisation, you should NEVER estimate the time needed based on your own effort, because ultimately you might not be the one ending up with the project, and whoever does will be short on time when performing the work. Conversely, if you are the slowest or most junior consultant in your team, resist the urge to estimate excessive time for the project, a small bit of pressure is conducive to growth and you will have your colleagues around you to help out a bit. When estimating effort, you should always aim for the average experience and skillset. That way, if your most experienced consultant reckon they can do the work in two days, and your most junior says 10 days, the right answer will likely be six days. For extra credit, you might even see if you can get your most experienced and most junior consultant assigned to the project together. This way, the experience will ensure that everything gets done, and the time allocation will ensure that there's time to share knowledge and teach.

While you can most certainly find bigger and more detailed models for estimating work in a book on "real" project management, the models described in the following have proved to be both pragmatic and sufficient in effectively estimating security consulting work for thousands of projects, without creating excessive overhead to the process.

Statistics

This might be the easiest and simplest way to estimate work, however it requires that you have a body of data to base it on. I originally started using this model when vulnerability scans and validating scanning results were the most popular service among clients, so I had an abundance of data and plenty of opportunity to test and verify it's accuracy. The same process can be used, if you are able to break down the steps or activities of a given service and measure how much time each step takes and how many times it needs to be repeated. That's just simple math. Here is the approach I took.

- At the time, we were offering two types of vulnerability scans, one for servers and one for web applications. The first step of the service was simple: setup the customer on the scanner, and configure the scan. This was a manual process if you were only doing a handful of servers, so I did the obvious thing; I timed myself doing it, 30 seconds. If it included a large group of servers, there was a more automated process, which I timed to 60 seconds (so if I needed to add more than two, the automated way would be faster).
- For web application scans, the initial setup had some advanced settings that

took more time, but for repeat customers that only needed to be done the first time. So I timed myself setting up a new scan (with the advanced settings) and a recurring scan. This was five and three minutes respectively.
- From our scanners, I collected the average number of vulnerabilities discovered per scan. Based on approx. 50.000 scans, the results were that for server scans there was an average of 9.9 vulnerabilities found per scan, and 31.6 vulnerabilities per web application scan.
- I then timed myself and a colleague verifying and validating 30 vulnerabilities discovered by our scanner, and averaged it out. This came to three seconds per finding.

At this time, I have enough numbers to create a basic calculus based on statistics. But I wanted to add in some more. So I looked at how much time was spent generating reports, how much time was spent coordinating with the customer, internal quality assurance processes, I even went and asked the sales department how much time was spent on average from lead to closing a scanning contract with a client. And I added all of these numbers to a spreadsheet, which resulted in this calculator:

Variable	Amount	Based on
Statistics		
Average number of vulnerabilities in a server scan	9.91	statistics based on 50300 scans
Average number of vulnerabilities in a web application scan	31.63	statistics based on 2621 scans
Personal timing		
Average time needed to verify a finding (in seconds)	3	personal timed action, averaged over 30 findings
Server scan		
Average time needed to configure a single server scan	30	personal timed action
Time needed to configure multiple server scans	60	personal timed action
Web application scan		
Average time needed to configure a single web application scan	120	personal timed action, where the settings already exists or is not needed
Average time needed to configure a single web application scan with advanced settings	300	personal timed action, creating the advanced settings
Planning and sales effort		
Project Management, coordinating with customers, etc.	3600	
Quality Assurance	600	
Sales time spent	5400	
Customers scope		
Hosts to be scanned	1337 <-- CHANGE THIS!	
Web applications to be scanned	37 <-- CHANGE THIS!	
Work-time for consultants for new customer	16.32	2.04
Work-time for consultants for existing customer	14.47	1.81
	Hours	**Days**
Work-time and sales-time for new customer	17.82	2.23
Work-time and sales-time for existing customer	15.97	2.00

The simple calculus was the average number of vulnerabilities in a scan, multiplied by the number of assets, multiplied by the average time needed to verify a finding, plus the one-time efforts of setup and sales.

And for the next 10 years, this is what I used when estimating this type of work. Every now and then, I'd go back and update the numbers. You can expand on this indefinitely, as long as you're able to qualify and quantify the steps involved in the work.

And the more data you have (projects, steps repeated, time spent) the more accurate these will be. You can use the same approach if you're doing post-exploitation engagements, provided you have a fixed set of activities you perform and a rough idea about how much time each activity takes. You can also apply this to software source code audits, by looking at the time spent setting up automated code auditing software, the number of results coming out of it, time spent validating them, or simply by timing how fast you read and understand a line of code and then multiply it by the number of lines in the entire codebase.

You can do this yourself, or you can do it with your entire team to get the true average of each of your activities. You can build calculators for specific services, or you can build them for specific outcomes (however that re. quires you to know the exact activities that need to be performed in order to guarantee that outcome). With services where a specific set of activities is almost guaranteed to provide a certain outcome, such models work really well. Here's an example of one for incident response and forensic services:

Investigation size			Small investigation		Medium investigation		Large investigation	
			Single hypothesis	Quantity	Three hypotheses or multiple assets	Quantity	3+ hypotheses or large estate	Quantity
Services included	Objective/Outcome	Activities included						
	First reponse and containment	Immidiate containment Evidence preservation guidance Incident management	3 consulting days	1	3 consulting days	1	3 consulting days	1
	Understand the root cause	Identify the source of the compromise Determine initial access	5 consulting days	1	10 consulting days	1	15 consulting days	1
	Identify data exfiltration or loss	Identify staging Identify data transfer or access	3 days per evidence source	3	3 days per evidence source	3	3 days per evidence source	3
	Understand if lateral movement took place	Determine scope of compromise	5 consulting days	1	15 consulting days	1	25 consulting days	1
	Deep Dive	All actions taken by the threat actor	3-5 days per evidence source	3	3-5 days per evidence source	3	3-5 days per evidence source	3
	Triage	Targeted acquisition Targeted artefact analysis	0,75 day per evidence source	5	0,75 day per evidence source	5	0,75 day per evidence source	5
	Incident management and support	Project management of investigation team Incident management Containment and remediation advice	0,5 day per day of investigation	12	1 day per day of investigation	12	1 day per day of investigation	12
Rates	Business hours		1 x day rate	1	1 x day rate	0	1 x day rate	0
	After hours		1.5 x day rate	0	1.5 x day rate	1	1.5 x day rate	0
	Weekends and holidays		2 x day rate	0	2 x day rate	0	2 x day rate	1
			Calculated effort:	40,75	Calculated effort:	91,1	Calculated effort:	151

While you can make similar calculators for things such as red teaming or general Assume Breach work, these should be made with larger margins or fudge factors due to the large degree of unknowns in such projects, however it should be possible to use statistics and calculus to produce rough estimates based on the work you whish to include in such a project.

Time-boxed

Time-boxing is the budget-friendly approach that most people don't like to talk about. It is not uncommon for a client to ask for a body of work, only to nearly pass out when you explain to them how much time it will take (and by extension how much it will cost). This is an unfortunate result of the general lack of knowledge on the buyers side about what goes into actual practical offensive or defensive security work (as opposed to security policy, governance, or engineering work, which is better understood and often more visible), and something you will need to embrace.

Usually, the normal estimation process looks like this:

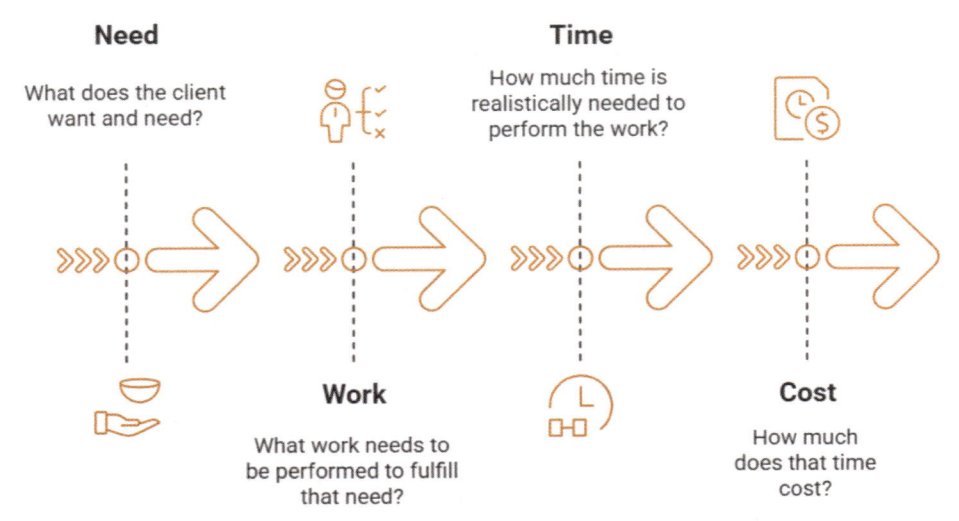

Need — What does the client want and need?

Work — What work needs to be performed to fulfill that need?

Time — How much time is realistically needed to perform the work?

Cost — How much does that time cost?

In a time-boxed approach, you turn it on its head and start from the opposite direction:

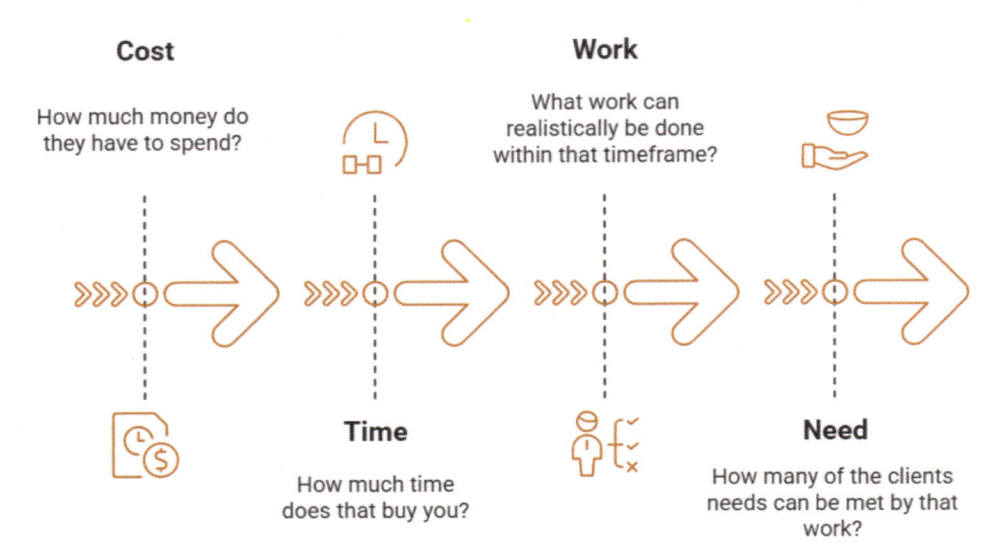

Cost — How much money do they have to spend?

Time — How much time does that buy you?

Work — What work can realistically be done within that timeframe?

Need — How many of the clients needs can be met by that work?

This makes it simpler for the client to simply put down how much money they have, and you can tell them how much work they can get for it. But realistically, a lot of clients don't want to tell you their real budget, so you might need to help them. My theory is that this is because a lot of consultancies will hear the budget, and then do everything they can to get as much of it as possible, instead of making sure that the customer gets exactly what they need. So whenever you get the impression that your estimate is too far removed from what the client was expecting to spend, suggest a time-boxed approach. Look at the body of work you feel needs to be performed in order to achieve the clients' stated objectives, and then shave it down to the smallest possible size where you still feel that you will be able to provide value by answering at least some of the clients questions and concerns, and then propose that amount as a time-boxed offering. In this fashion, you can tell the client that the smallest possible version of the assessment will be, for instance, five days, but that the cost of that reduction is that you will not be able to cover everything and that edge-cases might be omitted, or that the conclusion of the project may very well be that more work is needed. And the client has to be OK with that. You can then propose a slightly larger time-box, say for instance 8 days, which of course will give them more and better coverage, but you should still be honest to the client about the law of diminishing returns, and help them achieve as many of their objectives as possible within their budget.

In the context of technical consultancy work, the law of diminishing returns can be applied to the effort, time, or resources (like hiring more consultants or extending project hours) put into a particular project. Initially, adding more resources—whether it's time, money, or expertise—can lead to significant improvements and benefits. However, after a certain point, additional input often yields smaller improvements or value. In some cases, the added complexity or inefficiencies can even detract from the overall value.

When a consultancy team first begins, they can quickly identify and resolve key issues (e.g., system vulnerabilities, configuration problems, or security gaps). This is when the marginal return is high, as critical problems are addressed, and the client's situation improves rapidly. As more consultants or hours are added beyond a certain threshold, the incremental improvements become less impactful. The team may already have tackled the most critical issues, leaving minor or cosmetic improvements that do not deliver the same value. The cost of additional consultants or extended project time may exceed the actual value they bring.

Time-boxing should be used whenever there is a large gap between the budget of the client, and the amount of work that realistically needs to be performed to meet the clients' objectives. But it can also be used as optional components to an assessment. Examples of this are when a key component is the real focus of the clients' needs, but you in your scoping session determine that secondary components should also be tested to meet the objectives. In such cases, you can provide your best guess as to how much time is needed for the main components of the assessment, and then provide the client with the option of reviewing the secondary components either in full, or in a time-boxed fashion to keep the costs down, but still get an indication of the state of those components.

Representative testing

While not meant as a way of estimating work, representative testing can be used as a way to reduce amount of time needed while still providing a similar value to the client. The textbook example of this is the case where a client has one hundred computers and is in need of a security assessment to determine the security posture of all of them. Let's for a minute assume that you estimate that such an assessment will take three days of work per host. That's 300 days of work that the client will have to pay for. That estimate probably won't be accepted.

So a way to change the estimate is to ask the client any of the following:

- "How many of those computers are configured in the same way?"
- "Do you have a secure baseline you use to configure all of those computers?"
- "Is there a golden image that you use when deploying those computers?"
- "Can the computers be grouped together into similar roles and usage?"

What we're trying to understand is, is there a way for us to assess just a single host, and then extrapolate the results to multiple hosts? If they are all configured in the exact same way, then there is very little reason to test each and every one of them, if you can review one and then safely assume that the results will also apply to the rest. Or maybe you can review the golden image, or their configuration baseline to see if anything is missing? With this approach you might be able to change the estimate and scope of such a project from 300 days of mind-numbing repetitive low-value work, to the review of two or three different setups.

Programme or advisory work

Programme or advisory work are open-ended projects, where there may be an initial scope and estimate, but the real size of the project will very much be dependent on the results of the work performed. This is typical for projects such as gap-analysis or security improvement programmes, where you won't know what work needs to be done until you start doing it. The same applies to a lot of forensics and incident response work, or advisory work for when a new vulnerability is discovered and published and the client needs your expertise and advice as the situation develops.

For such projects, the real estimate is impossible to make, and the important thing is for you and the client to agree on rates, assign an initial amount of hours/days/cost, and establish an agreeable model for how and when you should inform the client that a pre-approved amount of time has been spent and more will be needed. If the work you are being asked for is something you've done before, then a safe bet is to have the initial estimate be similar to what you've used in the past, much like the statistics model discussed earlier. As a lot of your work may be invisible to the client, I would highly recommend that you keep track of your hours spent and what activities they were spent on, so that this can be shared with the client if they are surprised by the speed at which a pre-approved budget gets eaten up.

Pre-requisites

As discussed in The statement of work, the scope should also include any pre-requisites for making the project a success. After ending your meeting, with your understanding of the work that needs to be performed and the estimated time you will have available to you, determine what items are required for you to be able to carry out the work in the proposed time. Examples include:

- The timely delivery of user credentials
- Whitelisting/allowlisting in firewalls, IPS/IDS etc.
- Physical co-location with developers
- Access badges for onsite work to access relevant areas of the clients premises related to the assessment (for arrival, bathroom, coffee, cigarette breaks etc.
- API or application documentation, including documentation of authentication and authorization mechanisms, API methods, requests and responses with their expected parameters
- Machine-readable specifications such as Swagger or WSDL or Postman files
- Data set that can be used with the target in the appropriate environment, such as client IDs, card numbers etc.
- Sufficiently long timeout value on any authorization token used for testing, or temporary disabling of security features that might hinder automated security testing
- Architecture diagram of the target
- Baselines employed on assets to be assessed
- Source code and configuration files for the target solution
- Contact details of technical persons that can provide explanations on the workings of the application(s) to be tested
- Physical device required for testing in case of embedded systems or mobile solutions

- Onboarding onto cloud-assets
- Provisioning of Multi-Factor Authentication
- Integrated Development Environments with source code and dependencies
- Etc.

Pre-mortem

Pre-mortem analysis is a tool that lets you use your or your teams collective experience to predict problems in project, which ultimately should be factored into your estimates and your approach.

Pre-mortem analysis, a concept developed by Gary Klein, is a proactive strategy that helps teams predict potential failure points in a project before they occur. Unlike a traditional post-mortem, which examines what went wrong after a project fails, a pre-mortem asks the team or the individual to imagine that the project *has already failed*. By doing this, team members can explore all the reasons the project *could* have failed, but with the advantage that it hasn't actually happened yet. This freedom to brainstorm failure scenarios without fear of blame encourages honesty and creative thinking, helping to uncover risks that might otherwise be missed

In the book *Red Team Thinking* by Bryce G. Hoffman, the pre-mortem is positioned as a powerful tool for anticipating risks by forcing participants to think outside their usual optimistic tendencies. When you imagine a project has already failed, your brain shifts into a more cautious, realistic mode, leading to upwards of a 30% improvement in risk prediction. This approach also helps bypass groupthink, since the assumption of failure allows for bolder contributions from the team.

A pre-mortem analysis follows a structured process, often in a team setting, although it can also be done individually. Here's how you can run an effective pre-mortem:

- **Introduce the project**: Begin by clearly defining the project and its goals. Ensure all participants understand the purpose of the session—to anticipate failure scenarios and improve the project plan.
- **Set the scene**: Ask the team to imagine that the project has failed. The failure can be catastrophic or a minor setback, but the key is to focus on *why* it failed. This step opens the floor for creative, unconstrained thinking.
- **Brainstorm failure points**: Allow everyone to write down reasons for the project's failure. Encourage wild or silly ideas, as they often reveal unexpected insights. Whether it's technical difficulties, stakeholder disagreements, or external factors, all ideas should be captured.
- **Triage and prioritize**: After gathering the ideas, group similar risks and focus

on the most critical or likely scenarios. Participants can vote on which issues are most pressing, ensuring that the most probable and impactful risks are addressed first.
- **Plan preventive actions**: Once the key risks are identified, shift the focus to prevention. For each risk, discuss how the team can mitigate it, reduce its likelihood, or minimize its impact. This may include adjusting timelines, assigning additional resources, or preparing contingency plans.

Implement the solutions: Finally, document these preventive actions and ensure they are implemented. This step ensures that the insights gained from the pre-mortem translate into tangible changes that strengthen the project's resilience.

Applying Pre-Mortem to Improve Scoping and Estimation

By conducting a pre-mortem at the outset of a project, you can dramatically improve your scoping and estimation process. Here's how:

Enhanced risk awareness: By exploring possible failure points early, you gain a much clearer understanding of the risks involved in the project. This enables you to include buffer time and additional resources in your estimates, avoiding overly optimistic timelines

Refining the scope: Often, a pre-mortem reveals areas of the project that were either under- or over-scoped. For example, if the team identifies a complex feature or missing dependency that could derail the entire timeline, you can adjust the scope to handle that feature more cautiously, or even suggest postponing or eliminating it altogether.

Setting realistic expectations: Pre-mortem exercises often downplay optimism bias, forcing you to take a more realistic view of what can be achieved within the given constraints. This helps prevent underestimating the time, cost, or complexity of the project, leading to more accurate and achievable plans.

Benefits

Incorporating pre-mortem analysis into your project planning can dramatically reduce the chances of failure. By simulating potential failures before they happen, you can leverage the collective knowledge of your team to identify and address blind spots early, improve estimates, and set more realistic expectations with your client. Most importantly, it enables you to plan for the worst without the actual consequences of failure, leading to better outcomes and more successful projects overall.

Writing it all up

With all of the details now covered, it is time to write up your Statement of Work. Please refer back to the extensive (excessive?) example in chapter 1.

As discussed in chapter 1, 2 and 3, the scoping document needs to include enough details to let the client know what you will be doing, and convince them that this satisfies their needs. It also needs to contain enough details for colleagues to be able to determine if they have the pre-requisite knowledge to carry out the assessment, and let them or your future self know exactly what type of work is expected and the context and approach of said work.

While those chapters already covered this, it bears repeating that all scopes should include:

- The high-level purpose of the assessment. Why does the client need this test done?
- Overview of the scope of the assessment, broken into subsections if needed.
- Effort, how many consulting days will this cost?
- Any specific delivery requirements or non-standard deliverable formats?
- Pre-requisites needed for a successful engagement

And finally, ask your self, if you were presented with your writeup and no additional context, would you be able to carry out the assessment? If your answer is yes, then you have successfully scoped and written up your very own Statement of Work.

7. Closing thoughts

As should be clear by now, scoping can be both and art, and a science, depending on how you chose to approach it. As with anything, the more you practice it, the more artful, simple and easy it will seem to those around you. But until you reach that stage, having proven mechanics or a scientific approach to it, that allows you to measure and evaluate your success and failures, can serve as an invaluable safety net. This book has aimed to break down the complexities of the task, of defining your projects, of estimating the work that needs to be performed, and dealing with the many factors (human and otherwise) that go into arriving at a scope and formulating a structured project with actionable components.

My hope is that by reading this book, you have learned why scoping matters, how a well-defined scope prevents misunderstandings, reduces risk, and ensures a successful engagement for both consultant and client. You will hopefully also have learned or been reaffirmed in what to include, from statements of work and legal considerations to practicalities like defining scope boundaries, pre-requisites, and aligning expectations.

You will also have become more aware of who to have involved, the roles and responsibilities of consultants, clients, and supporting teams, and how clear communication can prevent misalignment and scope creep. This will also have tied into the question of when to scope, the importance of early-stage planning, real-world timing constraints, and the pitfalls of parallelized efforts and mismanaged resource allocation.

But most importantly, I hope that the contents of this book has helped teach you how to scope effectively, the step-by-step process of planning and running scoping meetings, asking the right questions, structuring documents, and aligning expectations with both technical and business stakeholders. Because that is the purpose with which I sat out to write this book; To provide you with practical and time-proven methodologies that will help you scope with confidence, regardless of the complexity of the engagement.

As you move forward in your career, I encourage you to apply these principles, refine them based on your experiences and the nuances of your area of our field, and continue to evolve your scoping practices. The cyber security landscape is ever-changing, and so too should our approaches to defining and planning our work.

A Final Thank You

Whether you are a consultant refining your approach or a client looking to improve how you engage with security professionals, I sincerely hope this book has given you valuable insights and tools to make scoping a smoother, more comfortable, predictable and enjoyable process, helping you to scope with confidence, precision, and expertise.

Scoping is often seen as an esoteric skill, but it doesn't have to be. With structured techniques and a clear understanding of objectives, constraints, and expectations, it can be transformed from a frustrating necessity into a strategic advantage. Remember, scoping is not just a preliminary step, it is the compass that guides your entire project. By mastering this skill, you're not only setting yourself up for success but also providing immense value to your clients and organization.

Thank you for taking the time to read this book. If this has helped you refine your approach to scoping, improve your engagements, or avoid a project disaster, then it has served its purpose.

Wishing you all the best in your future assessments. May your scopes be clear, your estimates accurate, and your projects successful.

Made in the USA
Las Vegas, NV
14 March 2025

19557584R00050